anniexpoetry

RUINED

Shade of

ROUGE

anniexpoetry

Writer's Pocket

First published by Writer's Pocket in 2024

email: publish@writerspocket.com

cover design by Khushi Desai

ISBN-13: 978-93-6083-197-4

www.writerspocket.com

ABOUT THE AUTHOR

Anushka Aswani is a young soul who dreams beyond scars.

She is a queer poet who shares her love with words and art. Her first poetry anthology, 'Ruined Shade of Rouge' walks through her childhood traumas, sufferings, and violent pain. Yet it expells her intense desires.

Anushka is a theist and a dreamer, a lover of beauty, roses, and simplicity. She has been broken, and now a part of her breathes in every person she has ever loved.

for my heart, which survived all the pain it didn't deserve,

and for the younger self, who taught me that
sometimes, the endings are better beginnings than the
beginnings themselves.

3:39 am

the nervous patterns of veins
i feel the cold chills down the spine!
unaware of what flows anxiously in the core
and what could unwind it…

do i really want to end it?
or conceal it under my concealer?
tangling thoughts,
and drowning dreams.

some haunting tune is there
my heart's lament; torturing me.
the silent echoes i hear
whispers the lost love of life.

tears that quietly flow
tells me i've been broken.
leaves me in a catastrophic hole
helpless and feeble.

what do i do with these feelings?
no escape; the grey shouts!
all i see,
a requiem for gone moments

CONTENTS

Enigmatic Existence

"she is a poetry herself"

Enigmatic Existence

between breaths and hopes, i barely survived.
i asked the universe; the enormous sky and the
cavernous ocean.
they whispered secrets i was too young to understand.

ENIGMATIC EXISTENCE

Twelve Secrets

he asked me about my fears
i hid them like i do with my tears.

i talked about the dark
deep water and it's shark;
maybe flying above the ground,
or someone's loud sound.

i lied my heart out
to ensure he doesn't go into doubt.
i didn't mention what scares me
i was afraid to take him into my sea.

putting them far away on the shelf
i counted them to twelvE

ENIGMATIC EXISTENCE

Till my Hands Bled

cried eyes
blurred sight
silk bed
the clock ticked to 3 a.m.

hurting seconds
bleak hours
unworthy days
played a show in blur.

i was breaking
piece after piece.
i sank painfully,
in my dead body.

in the memory
of forgotten sighs
i painted my words
red in colour.

i wrote
incessantly,
obsessively;
till my hands bleD

ENIGMATIC EXISTENCE

Wound

my wound is a dart
that stays with me as a part.
though; it tears me apart
i hold it in my heart.

i stay inside the bed
as if it's what is said.
dancing with the dead
my steps have turned red.

i am afraid of the day
and the moon makes me stay.
hopeless of any hopeful ray
the wound has paved my waY

ENIGMATIC EXISTENCE

The Dead

unknown of the light
i try to keep it all inside
bit of it i know
i must go with the flow.

the dead doesn't leave
and it drains my belief
i see horrible dreams
here, the thunder screams.

i left it on the shore
what i once wore
and as the night went by
i was left under the skY

ENIGMATIC EXISTENCE

The Emotionless Depths

here, the silence screams

a world of beauty it is
i am falling into a tête-à-tête with the waves.
there must be something ordinary in us
i could hear it talking deep secrets.

the ocean is terrifyingly beautiful
just as the person i see in the glass.
the frightening doesn't fright me
i suppose it's the part i belong to.

settling at the shore
i am waiting to hear some footsteps.
waiting for a sensational beauty
as if i want to be lost, yet to be found.

i wonder how we are connecting within,
strangely salty.
the extraneous is appealing and calm;
nevertheless, the core lies.

mysterious and mysterious, we are emotionlesS

ENIGMATIC EXISTENCE

Buried in the Stars

i wonder what this enormous sky hold
mysteries beneath; the stories untold
the bright blue shade, the black so close
folds the truth nobody knows.

the vast picture is a beauty with gleam
is it a dreamland or more than what it seem?
what must be beyond these clouds?
an infinite beauty? i doubt.

it holds two phases: dark and bright
the creation so ineffable, designs the velvet night
either this glowing art is god's divine grace
or some truth covered in the moon's cratered face.

what world and amazement exist there?
undefined, despite the ceaseless stare
a canvas of wonder; an ethereal expanse
sharing secrets in a cosmic dance.

there must be something; this sky knows
who watches over us? who is this close?
i have heard before, the ancient tale,
the immortal energy that lets us sail.

the picture, blank yet filled beyond what is seen by eyes
so i ask what lies beyond the skies
they say, there, heaven's angles play guitars
i conclude, the dark deep secrets buried in the starS

ENIGMATIC EXISTENCE

Find me in Them

i am broken.
and i wonder if anyone can ever find me
or where will they attempt to do this?

in the crowd of past?
in some beautiful pictures?
in restless nights?

i said i am broken.
i meant
in pieces.

there must be no place;
one can find me full
look carefully!

i have loved before.
insanely
countless times.

a piece of me;
still lies in every person
i have ever loveD

"she is a poetry herself"

Love

i define love in different terms.
for me, love is a sonnet written in our fates leading us
somewhere (nowhere).

Misery

all these times, made me a thing, a thing that doesn't
exist (doesn't deserve to exist).

Onsra

we know we aren't lasting
this mist will fade away soon
the most wanted relationship
will leave us forever broken.

knowing it from the depths
yet longing for it the most
the poignant rhythm, a pathetic song;
we always wanted to hear.

ephemeral like some winter month
but not falling into the next year
the smog of fading sighs
burns the eyes to red tears.

we sit on the edge of saying goodbye
holding each other.
watching the toughest hourglass
under the sad bluE

LOVE
Misery

14 February

a beautiful rose or a promise ring
perhaps the secret sorrow of cares.
a heart of belief or a shiny smile
perhaps the screams of silent tears.

not a love letter; not a red gesture
the moon conceals its dark side.
not a sky beneath the hues;
look, the flushed love day has died.

you may will to cross the ocean
meanwhile, love will blind you its depth.
you may wish for tranquility
meanwhile, love will hide you waiting wept.

the valentine wraps you a gift
excruciating pain and a scented knife.
the existing is the picture
too rough to realise the real life.

ain't nothing like antique lovers
the appealing mystique is a hallucination.
ain't the romance real
the modern touch is a blood celebratioN

LOVE
Misery

A Last Gift

it was a last gift from you
unwrapped; you handed me over
the soft fingers held it
as if it were a moon direct from the sky.

lately i realised it was poison
an art of killing me
gifting me the torturous pain
in the most sweetest way.

i take a burning gulp
with every running breath
its sore, or maybe worse than that
bleeding at a slight echo.

often i wonder, pray and desire
to take off this guilt
every time to realise it,
in a worsened waY

LOVE
Misery

I Write in the Grief of your Love

a lovely beginning it was
hand in hand; the promises made
shared smiles; rhymed the love
charmed eyes; dreamt of forever.

what we shared was a feeling
or maybe more than just what the picture showed
those tiny moments,
knitted the threads of our fondness.

the date we made together
and the fragile piece you wrapped around my neck
i had never felt so beautiful before
the charm in your eyes was unbelievable.

you gave me the purest of pure love
that exists in the fictional world
making me the fortunate one
to see the moon in the dark night.

i refuse to believe that you are gone
indeed, i turn down to our lost love
with dead hope
i write in the grief of your love.

beloved, your love denies to climb off my heart
with blood eyes, i stare at it
"all this was in the past"
a sigh i never moved on froM

LOVE
Misery

Mourning Streets

and here is another bleak hour
telling me to espouse the misery
just one more time,
one last (never-ending) time.

its hurting to hold onto the pain
as i am walking alone
on these empty streets
that mourns our love.

the flashbacks engulfing me
beneath a light lamp.
we are no longer us.
it was a less time when we fell apart.

despairing clouds hovering over
the drops could escape anytime!
and i fear the moist;
of our lost love.

cheers to this endless night!
grief filled to the brim
portraying the demise of our feelings
on the bare gloom skY

LOVE
Misery

Who made it Worse?

i realised when it hurt
knowing i can never heal
i wore the pain like a shirt
honestly, it made me seal.

it was the scar that made me afraid
the patient i was, the deeper it got
i believe the pain made me weighed
in the quite hours, i waited a lot.

it was tough to move on
the moments once gave me bliss, seemed a curse
the memories haunted of who i approved on
the person i welcomed with flowers made it worsE

LOVE
Misery

In the Multiverse

in this life,
we are not for each other
there are different paths
we must take.

we share the same sky
the glow of one moon
under alike stars
but can't see each other.

yet your heart is mine
and mine is yours
we are keeping this love
forever close.

nevertheless
in another world
our destinies are one
there, i have you.

in the multiverse, you are mine and i am yourS

LOVE
Misery

I will Always Remember You

i will always remember you
like a poetry
forever flowing in my veins
like some song
euphonious and eternal
like a favourite novel
closest to heart.

i will always remember you
like a beloved tale
beautifully written and directed
like a special verse
an unforgettable moment
like a loving melody
welcoming the spring.

i will always remember you
like a best-loved alliteration
sticks to the middle
like a caesura
rhyming the beats of heart
like a half-finished story
long forgotten rhythM

LOVE
Misery

Ring

a sign of promise,
keeping us close to forever
a ring or a symbol defining love's toll
the names scream alikeness.

a gem of no weight,
becomes the endless burden on heart
ironic how the hopes are put in a tiny circle
yet it becomes a story of sorrow.

a diamond; cold and heavy,
making love hard to bear
we wear our precious stone with faith
a cursed symbol, forever me and you.

a precious pearl,
blinding us from a trap of forever night
framing a future of loveless living
yours and mine.

the sphere is a pretty picture,
hiding the aching love in every story
each minute a promise turns to hurt
for a love thats all in vain

in the ring's tight grasp,
the story stays cold and lifeless
we are forever;
forever wearing love's cruel rinG

Desire

the extraordinary fantasies i live for, whispers a
seductive incantation.

Seduction

love me on tough days
desperate and intense.
wait for me
like trees wait for spring.

make yours what's mine
pain or pleasure.
hold my hands
make me your poetry.

be the sun
and i shall be the ocean.
darling!
let the evening celebrate our meetinG

LOVE
Desire

If I were a Poetry

if i were a poetry, you think you'd attend every word
dare to dive into the depths, every phrase carried
would you love to go through every stanza
would you judge the opening and every word i portray?

would you ask about the feelings the broken verses held
or be curious about the enjambments?
would you notice the concealed marks of shed tears
or be just another reader to me?

would you embrace me, or end me by my rhythm
would you look if i fascinated you
or are you courageous enough to go behind the archives
and see every flaw and beauty, every frown and grin?

would you want to rewrite me
replace some feelings somehow, or remove some
would you want to take up the pen to change the ending
and fall in love with me the way i fell in love with yoU

LOVE
Desire

Someone's Eyes, my Dream

a paradise i wanna see
in the real world
like some galaxies
colliding together.

an unbelievable beauty
as deep as an ocean.
the shades of brown,
and heavenly burnt umber.

the mesmerising eyes
i could never stop admiring
romantic beyond belief
a dream, to be seen by a wondeR

LOVE
Desire

Pain-ting

i wish he sees,
i wish he says

o my beloved
thou, like a painting
enchanting me
with beautiful colours.

you are delicately made
the mesmerising shades
perhaps traumas too
beautiful yet yelling agony.

you secrete thine archives
and i wish to undress you
see the naked soul
expelling the truth.

your tone lies here
darling, a mystery you are
like a pleasing painting
more, mourning pain.

coming closer a bit
my eyes are turning sore
as i dive into your strokes
you are truly a pain-tinG

LOVE
Desire

What is Forever?

the untold truth is here
forever is doom.

in the blurring dust of reality
we are hoping for the hopeless
all these dark clouds
but love clings to our soul.

we are believers
glossy eyes can't lie
wide smile of promises is true
heart sincerely beats for someone.

our love is posthumous
not a slave of breaths
it shall survive
here, or in the afterlife.

we promise forever to our fondness
above this boundless skY

LOVE
Desire

Welcoming the Love Again

oh dear love,
can you see it?
the bud is blooming again
an endeavour!

the dead melody of our song
practicing the tunes,
for you and me
to sing the love again.

the calm is beginning
through the rage and red,
paving the path
lighting the flames anew.

the distant past
gradually taking a side,
letting the warmth enter
awakening love.

our souls are dancing again
under the velvet sky,
rooting us in forever
like vines that twine.

we are growing afresh
stronger than before.
the moon is smiling,
the love is entwininG

"she is a poetry herself"

Childhood Cries

from waiting for a happy childhood to surviving the
torturous breakdowns,
bit by bit, i began to lose myself in the annals of time.

CHILDHOOD CRIES

Dear Mom

in the darkness of life
you left me giving a knife
like some gift, the tiny heart hid it
as if the piece wouldn't slit it.

years went by
and never did i calmly sigh
the time taught me the reason
as the gift changed life's season.

the fragile heart you left
unknowingly suffered a cleft
burdened by life's weight
let me ask: did you write my fate?

the torture is endless
making the nerves breathless
it's rough for my gentle hands
and it's the agony it demands.

mom, i am here. i beg of you
take me out of this blue
the knife is bloody, blurring the way
take your gift away, your pain awaY

CHILDHOOD CRIES

The Moon was Different when I was a Child

the moon smiled
when i saw it as a child
it has gone too away
miles far, it has made itself stay.

i adored the beauty of the moon
the way it hid from noon
just to appear at night,
hugging me with it's warmest sight.

it loved to bring a smile to my face
tiny eyes told me it was my safest place
now, the lone seems to be it's comfort
maybe to hide the part that's hurt.

too many beautiful mysteries
concealing some dreadful histories
a canvas of glorious flaws,
still a beauty making me pausE

CHILDHOOD CRIES

Happy Birthday?

a wish i heard late at night
looking at the shadow of flickering candlelight
the playback of traumas sat on my eyelids at ease
and all i repeated to torment was 'please'.

baloons danced, but my heart was torn in half
neither i cried, nor was it a real laugh
the cake bore the burden of wish
and some happy moments tried to swish.

i unwrapped golden gifts with silent cries
wished myself a happy birthday under sad eyes
welcomed another year of sobs in the still of night
figuring out whom to call to turn on the lighT

CHILDHOOD CRIES

Broken Fairytale

what i saw was a fairytale.

precise allure of white castle
the air scented lavender; blew mauve
candy floss clouds and their shimmery moves
sky with the charms of blue morpho.

the droplets of rain sat tenderly on the citadel
building the figures of my dreams
the stars fell in my favour
i was a princess wearing glass heels.

nevertheless, then i turned eleven.

the onset of darkness took place at the castle
atmosphere turned its ways
giving a sign of horrible thunder
it was the commencement of brutal truth.

pretty rain showered dead
the constellations drifted apart
the world was too harsh to hold my fingers
and my soft petals began to fall.

gradually, reality came to surface
the castle slowly dispersed
that world was just a will-o'-the-wisp
and real life; a misery i couldn't see.

amidst reality, the utopia submerged beneath mE

CHILDHOOD CRIES

Childhood: Not a Story of Joy

all i wanted to be was a daughter!
not a child filled in grief
all i wanted to be was a happy kid!
not a girl always staying in bed.

stop caring for me now!!
i have been hurt
stop touching these tears!!
when you couldn't give me warmth.

a child i was!!!
i didn't need to be taught!
a child who starved for love!
i needed to be protected!!!

all my life,
i have screamed silently
all my pain
kept praying to be better!

i am still here;
recovering from these traumas
i am still wondering
why i just couldn't be as happy as other kidS

something ended in me
to begin somethinG

Writer's Pocket

Writer's Pocket is a publication house established in 2016. We began with the aim of providing a better publishing platform for aspiring writers and budding poets.

The publishing industry in India (and around the world, to a great extent) is always something of a mystery even to the writers themselves. We are working on making publishing more accessible to everyone.

So far, we have helped over 3,000 writers turn their dreams into reality by publishing the books and continue to do so. By doing so, we also provide some of the best content by Indian writers to the readers.

Want to read more books? Scan this QR code with your smartphone and check out all our books on Amazon.